Conservation and the C̶o̶u̶n̶t̶r̶y̶s̶i̶de:

Mark Pennington

Published by the
IEA Environment Unit

1996

First published in April 1996
by

THE ENVIRONMENT UNIT
THE INSTITUTE OF ECONOMIC AFFAIRS
2 Lord North Street, Westminster,
London SW1P 3LB

Studies on the Environment No.6

ISBN 0-255 36379-6

Cover design by David Lucas

Set in Plantin and Univers
Printed in Great Britain by
Goron Pro-Print Co Ltd, Lancing, W. Sussex

Table of Contents

Foreword

If one needed to think of a British equivalent to the American 'motherhood and apple pie' – something that everyone unthinkingly supports – it would be the countryside. This sentimental unanimity is well illustrated by the joint letter to *The Times* in February 1996 from the three main party leaders, John Major, Tony Blair and Paddy Ashdown, in which they 'gladly [took] the opportunity of showing that on one subject [they spoke] with a united voice – namely in advocating the protection of our countryside in its rich personality and character'.

But what does the protection of the countryside mean? We all wish to protect motherhood and apple pie, but not all mothers and every apple pie. Some children need to be protected from their mothers and many apple pies stand in considerable need of improvement rather than protection. Yet the British attitude seems to be that the countryside ranks even higher than motherhood and apple pie, and should be protected on all occasions and in all circumstances – whatever it looks like, apparently it displays its rich personality and character and the people should be called on to protect it from any threat. But this universal sympathy is, in itself, a danger. Just because it is unthinking and unquestioning it can be manipulated to serve other ends by those who stand to gain from change in the apparently unchanging character of the countryside. For the countryside does change, and the English countryside is, as many others have remarked, largely man-made in its characteristics. It therefore changes as people respond to social, economic and technological change.

The letter of February 1996 marked the 70th anniversary of the founding of the Council for the Protection of Rural England (CPRE), and also consciously echoed a similar letter to *The Times* in May 1929 signed by Stanley Baldwin, Ramsay Macdonald and David Lloyd George, also at the instigation of the CPRE. But at the time the CPRE was founded Stanley Baldwin could speak of:

'The sounds of England, the tinkle of the hammer on the anvil in the country smithy, the corncrake on a dewy morning, the sound of the scythe against the whetstone, and the sight of a plough team coming over the brow of a hill, the sight that has been seen in England since England was a land, and may be seen in England long after the Empire has perished and every works in England has ceased to function, for centuries the one eternal sight of England.'[1]

But these sights and sounds have all vanished, as has the Empire, and most of the works, because of economic, political and technological change. And the changes which have caused the disappearance of the sights and sounds of the countryside which Baldwin portrays have been speeded by government policies towards farming, encouraging increased production at the expense of the apparently eternal.

Government policies affect the countryside even when the effects are not intentional. They alter what the countryside is, affecting it for the better and for the worse, and it is the rôle of government with respect to the countryside which is Mark Pennington's concern. For government is not neutral. Its policies are subject to capture by interested parties and, because of people's unthinking support for 'the countryside', the policies are paradoxically easier to capture. The protection of the countryside can too easily be transmuted into protection and support for those who work and/or live in the country, and they can impose their interests on policies, assuring the urban population that they are the guardians of the countryside so that doing so therefore protects the countryside. So the Town and Country Planning Act of 1947 excluded farm buildings from control. Farming policies encouraged the grubbing up of hedges, increasing output at the expense of bird life and of the apparently eternal image of the English field system.

More recently, policies have been drawn up which are explicitly intended to protect the countryside but, as Mark Pennington shows, these may then be operated in the bureaucratic interest of the agencies which put them into effect. Policies designed to encourage the conservation of species and habitats can conflict with policies designed to increase

---

[1] Quoted in *The Times* ('Rare show of unity as party leaders go to the country'), 9 February 1996, p.2.

agricultural production, necessitating further bureaucratic intervention to remedy the situation.

The general predisposition in favour of the countryside can be manipulated and distorted until it is not clear that the policies which are put into operation actually achieve the desired end, whatever the stated intention. So, in the end, it is clear that there is only one kind of action which will be universally condemned as failing to protect the countryside, and that is the construction of new, non-agricultural buildings. Other changes which might alter the balance of nature may be accepted, only development will not be, even when, for example, a low-density housing development would encourage a wider diversity of species than the agricultural mono-culture it might replace.

Mark Pennington exposes these issues with an incisive critique of rural policies and policy-making. He also suggests an alternative kind of rural policy. Readers will gain a clear understanding of the problems, the nature of which I have sketched out in this Foreword. To what extent we could extricate ourselves from the situation he describes without also having to extricate ourselves from the Common Agricultural Policy and hence from the European Union, I leave it for the reader to decide.

February 1996   ALAN W. EVANS
Professor of Environmental Economics and
Deputy Vice-Chancellor, University of Reading

*Professor **Evans**'s recent research has been concerned with the economics of town planning. His book* No Room! No Room! The Costs of the British Town and Country Planning System, *was published by the IEA in 1988 as Occasional Paper No. 79.*

Preface

This is the first book in the Environment Unit's series which specifically concentrates on the public choice school of analysis. For too long economists have recommended government intervention without having a model of how government actually works. As Mark Pennington shows, when bureaucratic incentives are analysed governmental intervention is often worse than the market 'failure' it is supposed to alleviate.

The IEA Environment Unit is delighted to offer this pathbreaking book. The views expressed are those of the author, not of the Institute (which has no corporate view), its Trustees, Advisers or Directors.

February 1996   ROGER BATE
                              Director, IEA Environment Unit

The Author

Mark Pennington has a BA in Geography from Royal Holloway College, University of London, and is currently pursuing a PhD at the London School of Economics and Political Science, University of London. His thesis employs the principles of public choice and modern theories of property rights to examine the release of land for residential development under the British town and country planning system.

In 1994 Mr Pennington was a Summer Research Fellow at the Institute for Humane Studies at George Mason University, and in March 1995 became a Research Fellow of the IEA Environment Unit.

Acknowledgements

I take this opportunity to thank a number of people for their help in the preparation of this paper: my colleagues at the LSE, Penny Law and Dan Graham; Roy John of the Country Landowners' Association; Dr Yvonne Rydin; Vicky Rea; the staff at the IEA Environment Unit, especially Roger Bate, Julian Morris, Lisa Mac Lellan and Professor Colin Robinson; Professor Alan Evans; Dr Matt Ridley; and two anonymous referees. I am also most grateful to Sir Chips Keswick and Lord Vinson of Roddam Dene LVO for supporting this project. Special thanks go to my mother.

Finally and most of all, I would like to thank John and Christine Blundell for their help and encouragement over the last two years, and the Institute for Humane Studies, without whose financial support most of my postgraduate work would not have been possible.

Any errors within the text are mine and mine alone.

February 1996   M.P.

Introduction

Before the Second World War, countryside conservation in the United Kingdom rested with individuals and voluntary bodies. From the natural history societies of the Victorian middle classes, to the first property obtained by the National Trust, conservation was a matter for the private sector. Half a century of government control began with the 1947 Town and Country Planning Act, which removed from the individual the automatic right to develop land, paving the way for Green Belts, National Parks and the other statutory designations which have become the dominant feature of countryside policy.

In recent years, site designation has been mirrored by conservation expenditures, through a labyrinth of quangos[1] and bureaucracies, but the growing list of government controls appears not to have revived the fortunes of the rural environment. Conservationists lament the removal of hedgerows, farmers demand greater subsidies to conserve the vestiges of landscape, yet to be converted to arable desert, while the loss of flora and fauna continues unabated.

Environmental decline has led inexorably to pressure for even stricter controls to preserve 'biodiversity'. The White Paper, *This Common Inheritance* (1990), and the Planning and Compensation Act (1991) make an explicit commitment to countryside protection, the latter hailed by a Council for the Protection of Rural England (CPRE) spokesperson as 'One of the most important pieces of environmental legislation in the past twenty years' (Burton,1991, p.70).[2]

Against this backdrop, there are competing visions of conservation policy. The dominant view attributes countryside destruction to 'market failures' and proposes a régime of

---

[1] 'Quango' is the term used for quasi-autonomous non-governmental organisations. These bodies are state-appointed boards employed to implement elements of government policy. They are nominally separate from the agencies of central government but still constitute an arm of the state bureaucracy, with discretionary decision-making powers.

[2] Tony Burton is a senior employee of the Council for the Protection of Rural England.

centralised planning, operated by benevolent managers to maximise 'environmental welfare'. This paper challenges the conventional wisdom, arguing that government control, far from a cure for the ills of the countryside, is actually the cause of the disease.

Public choice theory recognises the importance of human self-interest and suggests that where the motives of bureaucrats, politicians and interest groups are not constrained by institutional incentives, 'government failure' is pervasive. It is the contention of this paper that the history of countryside policy represents a catalogue of bureaucratic mismanagement and special-interest manipulation. Conservation depends on an end to political interference and a return to full private property rights.

The argument is divided into three parts. Section 1 outlines the importance of institutions and in particular the lack of appropriate incentives within the political sphere. Sections 2 to 5 use the theory of public choice to examine the patterns of bureaucratic and interest-group control over conservation policy. Finally, the concluding pages examine the prospects for environmental improvement in the countryside under a property rights alternative.

1. Market Failure or Government Failure?

The Importance of Institutions

The study of environmental decision-making, like any other sphere of economic analysis, must account for the self-interested nature of human kind. Human self-interest may be pecuniary or non-pecuniary in motivation, but people will always calculate costs and benefits when making their personal choices.[1] Incentives matter above all and a successful policy is more likely to be one which works with the grain of human nature.

The successful stewardship of resources depends on the institutional setting in which self-interested behaviour is to occur. If efficiency entails the co-ordination of people's actions to achieve mutually compatible goals,[2] then differing arrangements vary in their capacity to achieve this aim. Institutions which allow individuals to reap the rewards and to bear the costs of their actions and which transmit information about these decisions, will be advantageous from the viewpoint of the individual and society. Where institutional defects allow costs to be passed on to others, where wealth is not dependent on the nature of decisions made and where there is a lack of information, efficient resource allocation is less likely to result (Libecap, 1989, and North, 1990).

Conventional analyses of countryside conservation have found markets and private property to fail the institutional test. Welfare economists in particular argue that property owners are not held to account for their actions. 'Spillover' effects

---

[1] It is just as much an act of self-interest to pursue religious or other beliefs such as countryside conservation, as it is to engage in the pursuit of money, especially if one seeks to impose the consequences of these beliefs on other individuals.

[2] According to Israel Kirzner, an economic process is efficient to the extent that it harmonises the plans of individuals in the pursuit of their goals. This definition is particularly appropriate to a 'comparative institutions' approach. It does not require that a process is 'perfect' as in many welfare economics and equilibrium theories, but rather that it facilitates co-ordination in a superior way to other institutional frameworks. The significance of this approach will become apparent when comparing the 'efficiency' of government and market in Section 6 of this paper (see Kirzner, 1992).

associated with private decisions and the divergence between private and social costs are deemed as instances of 'market failure' (Baumol and Oates, 1975).[3]

The creation of an attractive landscape through traditional farming methods will be 'underproduced' because the 'public good' characteristics of a scenic landscape mean that people may consume the benefits irrespective of payment. Similarly, urban developments on green field sites fail to account for the 'negative externalities' in their provision, so restrictions on the rights of property are required to correct for the defects of the market system.

The market failure approach is entrenched in environmental policy-making, but, save for sophisticated guesswork, its adherents neglect to explain how planners and government bureaucrats are to 'correct' for the alleged 'imperfections'.[4] Profits and losses in the market provide a measure of efficiency, but bureaucratic decision-making is not subject to any test of success in correcting market failures. Nor is such a measure possible under central planning, for without prices there is no way to discover the dispersed evaluations of consumers. As Hayek (1948, p.77) argues:

> 'Data from which the economic calculus starts are never for the whole society "given" to a single mind which could work out all the implications and can never be so given.'

Moreover, the market failure theorists neglect the potential for self-interested behaviour by governmental actors. Environmental bureaucrats assume the mantle of disinterested experts, selecting the appropriate regulations to maximise environmental welfare. Government departments, it would seem, are populated by

---

[3] Baumol and Oates (1975) is typical of the welfare economics approach.

[4] Sophisticated guesswork usually takes the form of social/cost-benefit analysis. The fundamental difficulty with cost-benefit analysis is the assumption of a common scale of values upon which all decisions can be ranked and aggregated to reach a quantitative 'social' figure. Cost, however, is an entirely subjective concept and cannot be measured by anyone other than the chooser: aggregation is impossible (see Formaini, 1991). Even if this problem could be resolved (which it cannot), there would still be the problem of obtaining the information concerning the values necessary for the aggregation. Since these are dispersed throughout the population there is no way a cost-benefit planner could ever attain the information.

motiveless 'economic eunuchs' (Buchanan, 1978, p.11). In fact, when we add to the informational difficulties of central planning the reality of self-interested behaviour, there is a recipe for government failure surpassing anything the market might deliver.

The Anatomy of Government Failure

Government failure is a product of perverse incentives in the political process which are largely to the benefit of politicians, interest groups and bureaucrats.

Interest groups lobby for subsidies and regulations, the benefits of which are concentrated on their members, as when producers in a domestic industry lobby for the imposition of import quotas. Most voters, however, lose only a small amount through legislation, for example in higher prices, and the costs of mobilising the dispersed mass of voters in a countervailing organisation are far too high (Buchanan and Tullock, 1982, and Tullock, 1989). Thus, even where regulations are not the product of interest-group demands, it is more than likely that they will be 'captured' and manipulated by those being regulated (Stigler, 1975).

In addition, it is perfectly rational for most voters to remain 'ignorant' of policy consequences, because the cost of acquiring accurate and detailed political information when so many issues are decided via the ballot box, is prohibitive given the miniscule chance of each voter being decisive in an election. Consequently, vote-seeking politicians, considering the short-term goal of re-election, respond to the demands of concentrated interest groups, dispersing the costs across the rest of the population (Downs, 1957, Buchanan and Tullock, 1982, Tullock, 1989, and Seldon, 1993).[5]

The bureaucratic agencies which supply subsidies and regulations are not directly responsible for the costs of their actions; they rely on budget appropriations rather than risking their own or shareholders' capital. Because bureaucrats do not make profits and losses there are no incentives to allocate resources according to any criterion of economic success.

---

[5] The process by which interest groups lobby for government subsidies and favourable regulations is often referred to as 'rent seeking' in the public choice literature.

15

Rather, the success of the bureaucrat is measured in terms of job security, status and rank, which may be largely dependent on the size of the bureau budget. Budget-maximising bureaucrats support policies and interest groups which are favourable to budgets, irrespective of the true demand for their services and any external effects (Niskanen, 1971, Baden and Stroup, 1981, and Blais and Dion, 1991).[6]

Interest-group and bureaucratic control are the epitome of 'government failure', which, as the following pages show, has been the defining feature of countryside policy throughout the post-war period.[7]

---

[6] There is still dispute concerning the extent to which bureaucrats do maximise their budgets. For example, Professor Patrick Dunleavy (1991) argues that civil servants working in bureaus where the bulk of any spending increment flows outside the agency – such as a social security bureau inscribing higher values on welfare cheques, paid to a fragmented clientele of welfare consumers – have few incentives to increase the size of the budget. According to Dunleavy, bureaucrats will tend only to maximise that part of the budget held within the bureau for staffing and administration. Alternatively, civil servants might also maximise transfer payments if these are destined for a highly organised interest group, operating in a corporatist relationship with the bureau and well able to organise a flowback of benefits to senior officials in exchange for greater subsidies. All the bureaus discussed in this paper fall into the categories where budget increments are spent within the bureau (planning bureaucracies and conservation quangos), or are transfer/subsidy payments paid to a highly organised interest group (agricultural and forestry bureaucracies), so the budget maximisation thesis is appropriate.

[7] The following apply the public choice approach to the politics of environmental decline in the United States: Anderson (1982), Baden and Fort (1980), Baden and Stroup (1981), Baden and Leal (1990), Deacon and Johnston (1985), Libecap (1981).

2. Farmers, MAFF and the Countryside, 1947-1981

Planning Control :
Environmental or Agricultural Protection?

The two pieces of legislation which set the historical backdrop to government failure in the countryside were the 1947 Town and Country Planning Act and the Agriculture Act of the same year. Both of these provide object lessons in special interest and bureaucratic manipulation which is the inevitable result of political control over private property rights.

The Town and Country Planning legislation established the framework for the designation of special environmental sites, such as Green Belts, Areas of Outstanding Natural Beauty (AONBs) and National Parks, which were to become the hallmark of countryside policy in subsequent years. This was facilitated by a massive transfer of property rights from private individuals to the state, where private ownership was maintained, but development rights were transferred to local authority planning departments and the Ministry of Housing and Local Government (since 1970 the Department of the Environment). Thereafter, anyone wanting to develop his or her property had to apply to the local authority for planning permission which would be approved or rejected according to a local development plan. The magnitude of this change is captured eloquently by two leading planning lawyers:

> 'It is impossible to exaggerate the importance of July 1st 1947 from the viewpoint of the local planning authority, the landowner or the building developer, for the 1947 Act conferred some of the most drastic and far reaching provisions ever enacted, affecting the ownership of land and the liberty of the owner to develop and use his own land. Indeed, after 1947 ownership of land carries with it nothing more than the right to go on using it for existing purposes' (Grant and Heap, 1991).

The Agriculture Act 1947, meanwhile, began an era of unprecedented support to the farming sector, even before entry into the European Common Agricultural Policy in 1973. The main mechanism was the setting of guaranteed prices for virtually all staple products by the Ministry of Agriculture, Fisheries and Food (MAFF) and the National Farmers Union (NFU). With further support for machinery, fertilisers and land drainage, the subsidised régime provided for a doubling of farmer's incomes by the mid-1970s (Bowers and Cheshire, 1983).

It is often thought that the introduction of planning controls and site designations was primarily an act of environmental policy, but in practice this was never the case. In reality, the town planning legislation was inextricably linked to the new régime of subsidised farming. The first Green Belts, AONBs and other designations were judged of crucial significance in stemming the tide of urban encroachment, which was seen by many as the principal threat to the countryside, but the emphasis was always on the 'protection of agricultural land' rather than countryside conservation *per se*.

This was not surprising given the political power of the farming lobby, for if ever an act of government was the product of interest group manipulation it was the Agriculture Act. As Howarth (1990) argues, there can be no explanation for the Labour government providing generous subsidies to capitalist farmers, other than a belief on its behalf that a concentrated block of votes might be won. With farmers highly concentrated in large rural constituencies, a one in four swing in the agricultural vote could have delivered 19 seats to either of the major parties in 1955. Thus, even if the initial support was based on a desire to avoid food shortages in the immediate aftermath of the War, only the strength of the farmers could account for the political competition in subsequent years to expand the subsidised régime.[1]

Likewise, the farmers were the dominant force in the coalition for urban planning controls, with the predominantly tenant members of the NFU standing to lose their holdings if agricultural land was converted to alternative uses. Subsidised

---

[1] Howarth also notes the disproportionate representation of farming interests in parliament: about 10 per cent of Conservative members held farming interests even though farmers accounted for only 0.2 per cent of the total electorate.

agriculture and protected tenancies were the driving force behind the nationalisation of development rights, and in a classic example of regulatory capture, agricultural uses such as farm buildings, fences and hedgerow grubbing were exempt from the planning permissions which were standard for other developments. It was equally the political clout of the farmers which resisted the socialist desire to nationalise the ownership of land itself. The control of development rights allowed farmers to maintain control over the production process and to protect the agricultural sector, without becoming totally dependent on the state regarding day-to-day farm decisions.

Budget maximisation was also well to the fore, with the budgetary interests of the MAFF firmly linked to the expansion of the subsidised sector. If more land was taken for non-agricultural development, the power of the farmers and the size of the agricultural budget would decrease and with it the discretionary grant-giving of MAFF bureaucrats. Thus, local authorities were required to consult the MAFF when considering planning applications leading to the loss of 2 hectares or more of agricultural land, and with 10 per cent of councillors in the shire counties employed in farming, most planning committees were dominated by representatives of the farming lobby (Herington, 1984).

Given the environmental disaster which was to result from the expansion of subsidised agriculture, it should be a salutary lesson for contemporary environmentalists who claim superior foresight with regard to conservation, that the then representatives of the CPRE and the Royal Society for the Protection of Birds (RSPB), although electorally weaker, supported the farmers in the coalition for subsidies (Lowe *et al.*, 1986).[2] To the conservationists the principal threat to the countryside came from urban development and they argued that agricultural subsidies would provide the cheapest and most effective way of conserving the rural landscape. This, despite the fact that as early as 1942, the economist Professor S.R. Dennison, a member of the 1942 Scott Committee on Rural

---

[2] The CPRE had no formal national membership structure during this period and membership of the RSPB was only 7,000 in 1955 (see Annual Reports). The NFU meanwhile had over 200,000 members (see Howarth, 1990).

Land Use, was already predicting the disastrous consequences of a subsidised, mechanised agriculture (Lowe *et al.*, 1986, pp.16-17).

The Environmental Impact of Agricultural Support[3]

Throughout the 1950s and 1960s farm prices were set well above the prevailing world market level and the plethora of machinery grants, land drainage programmes and subsidised fertilisers combined to encourage agricultural specialisation, in particular for cereal production and a process of intensification.

With subsidy payments related positively to the level of production, land prices rose substantially as the possession of agricultural land became, in effect, 'a licence to receive subsidies' (Cheshire, 1983, quoted in Howarth, 1990). Higher prices raised the real cost of land above that of labour and heavily subsidised capital inputs. Thus, farmers intensified their use of land, which usually meant the removal of hedgerows, the adoption of 'prairie farming' techniques, massive use of chemical fertilisers and pesticides, and an insatiable appetite for the conversion of marginal areas. All of these effects were intensified with the still greater subsidies under the CAP, but it is important to realise that much of the damage was already done before British entry in 1973 (Bowers and Cheshire, 1983).

Between 1945 and 1970, 1 per cent of hedgerows (8,000 km.) were removed annually, amounting to a cumulative loss of 225,000 km. These losses were concentrated in the cereal growing areas, with counties such as Norfolk losing over half of their stock and the population of field birds such as corn buntings, corncrakes, grey partridges and larks suffering heavy losses as a direct result (Lowe *et al.*, 1986, pp.65-66).

The extension of agriculture into more marginal lands was particularly devastating for chalk grassland and heathland environments. Over 80 per cent of chalk grassland disappeared after 1949 as huge areas of downland in Southern England were ploughed and sprayed with chemical fertilisers and pesticides. The result was a dramatic decline in butterfly populations, with

---

[3] Bowers and Cheshire (1983), Munton (1983) and Lowe *et al.* (1986) provide the best review of the environmental effects of farm support.

marbled whites, chalkhill blues and brimstones some of the worst sufferers. In the case of heathland, over 60 per cent was destroyed with a concurrent decline in the fortunes of lizards and the virtual elimination of the smooth snake (Lowe *et al.*, 1986, p.68).

In addition, large areas of moorland were converted to agricultural use, with substantial tracts of Exmoor and other uplands disappearing under the plough, whilst the continued presence of hill farming subsidies encouraged over-grazing. Meanwhile, the massive use of subsidised fertilisers led to a deterioration of soil structure, especially in Eastern England, where leaching of nutrients resulted in the eutrophication of many streams and waterways.[4]

The wetlands were the principal victims of the MAFF drainage and reclamation schemes with about 50 per cent of lowland fens, mires and valleys destroyed or badly damaged by the early 1980s. This was a catastrophe for field-nesting birds such as the snipe, redshank, lapwing and the yellow wagtail (Lowe *et al.*, 1986, pp.66-67).

Undoubtedly, some of these changes would have occurred irrespective of agricultural support, but the sheer scale of the destruction owed everything to the power of the farming lobby to extract ever greater subsidies (£40 billion between 1947 and 1982 at 1982 prices, according to Body, 1983) from the consumer. Most important, however, and contrary to popular opinion, the threat to the countryside from urban encroachment could never have been as great as the damage inflicted by agriculture. Thus, in the absence of planning controls and subsidies, even if the pre-war rates of agricultural to urban conversion (25,000 hectares per annum) had been maintained, the proportion of land in urban uses would still not have reached 20 per cent and the resulting loss of habitat could hardly have

---

[4] Leaching is the term used to describe the process by which, as soil structure deteriorates, usually due to the loss of humus caused by repeated cultivation, nutrients and minerals are washed through the soil profile rather than held between the soil particles. Eutrophication refers to the process whereby nitrogen-based fertilisers, having been washed through the soil profile or having drained off the fields, increase the nutrient content of streams and waterways to such an extent that they become clouded with large algal blooms.

competed with the destruction due to subsidised farming.[5] Indeed, the position for birds and wildlife would have been considerably better, because much of the urban development would have consisted of garden space, which is much more favourable than arable deserts.

In short, 'market failure' through urban development could never have been a match for 'government failure' in agricultural policy. Habitat loss in the post-war era was the product of large-scale wealth transfers and the manipulation of planning controls and site designations by the farming lobby. Benefits were concentrated on farmers and MAFF bureaucrats with the costs, both pecuniary and environmental, dispersed across an unsuspecting populace.

---

[5] At present approximately 1·64 million hectares of England and Wales or 11 per cent of the total land area is devoted to urban uses. (One hectare is equivalent to just under 2·5 acres.) Even if the rate of rural-to-urban conversion had continued at 25,000 hectares per annum, which is highly unlikely (the current rate is 5,000 hectares), the urban area today would be about 19 per cent. Habitat loss due to an extra 8 or 9 per cent conversion would not have been as great as the +50 per cent due to agricultural support. For rural to urban conversion figures see Cullingworth and Nadin (1994).

3. Conservation and the Quango State

If the farming lobby was the dominant force throughout most of the post-war period, the 1980s saw the rise of the environmentalists[1] and an explosion of new site designations and subsidy schemes, managed by a complicated web of government agencies and quasi-autonomous bodies. Predictably, the imperatives of interest-group and bureaucratic manipulation have not been thwarted by the extension of the quango state and the continuing evidence of environmental failures points to perverse incentives in the quangocratic régime.

Nature Conservation[2]

Between 1949 and 1991 nature conservation was the responsibility of the Nature Conservancy (Nature Conservancy Council (NCC) since 1973), a quango attached to the Department of the Environment (DoE). Following the 1990 Environmental Protection Act, the NCC was split into its constituent parts with separate agencies for Scotland, Wales and England. Scottish Natural Heritage and the Countryside Council for Wales combine nature conservation with the broader goal of landscape management, whereas English Nature continues to focus on natural history concerns.[3]

The Nature Conservancy was awarded the Royal Charter in 1949 and obtained its powers following the National Parks and

---

[1] Membership of environmental groups has increased dramatically over recent years. For example, RSPB membership increased from 7,000 in 1955 to 321,000 in 1980 and to 800,000 by 1990 (see RSPB Annual Reports). Friends of the Earth had 10,000 members in 1970 but by 1993 this figure had grown to 120,000 (see Annual Reports).

[2] Nature conservation refers specifically to the management and study of flora and fauna within special sites and is distinct from the broader issues concerned with landscape and amenity.

[3] Given this highly complex structure I refer mostly to the NCC and English Nature. Any references post 1990 for nature conservation, unless otherwise stated, implicitly include the Scottish and Welsh bodies. The landscape management role in England is peformed by the Countryside Commission and MAFF (see below, pp.28-34).

Access to the Countryside Act of the same year. This enabled the purchase or lease of land for National Nature Reserves and the designation of Sites of Special Scientific Interest (SSSIs).[4] SSSIs remained in private ownership, but local authorities were required to take into account the designated status when considering planning applications of a non-agricultural nature.

Conservation policy grew rapidly following the Wildlife and Countryside Act 1981, which was the British response to a 1979 EC Directive on the conservation of wild birds. The passage of this Act focused attention on depredations in the countryside and, in particular, the rapid loss of SSSIs due to agricultural intensification. In Kent, for example, almost 2,500 hectares of biological SSSI were lost to agriculture between 1968 and 1979 (Barton and Buckley, 1983).

With agriculture excluded from planning controls, the environmental lobby headed by CPRE and RSPB, having finally recognised the folly of subsidised farming, complained that designated sites had little protection and demanded new powers for the NCC to maintain the existing stock. After a pitched battle between the environmentalists and the farmers,[5] the eventual outcome was a new system of 'management agreements' and protective controls.

Management agreements are offered to landholders (usually farmers) as compensation for loss of income due to SSSI designation. They originated under Section 15 of the Countryside Act 1968, but the 1981 legislation extended their remit, preventing owners from damaging sites until the NCC had the chance to enter negotiations. Some sites became subject to even stricter control under a DoE Nature Conservation Order and failure to reach SSSI agreement may lead to compulsory purchase.

---

[4] There are two main types of SSSI: biological, which includes special flora and fauna, and geological, which contains special geomorphological features such as limestone pavements.

[5] Lowe et al. (1986) provides an excellent discussion of the lobbying process for the Wildlife and Countryside Act and its amended version in 1985. The amended version prevented landowners from damaging SSSIs during the three-month period after initial consultation, but before the notification actually took effect, and thus closed what was known in the legislative jargon as the 'three-month loophole'.

Following Section 28 of the Wildlife and Countryside Act, all SSSIs had to be re-notified and documented in detail to facilitate monitoring by the NCC. It is difficult to imagine a government policy more riddled with incentives for bureaucratic expansion.

With bureaucratic status and security of employment linked to the overall size of the nature conservation budget, there are few incentives rewarding bureaucrats for the good stewardship of the resources under their control. Indeed, it can be argued that the more damage to environmental sites, the more likely it is for bureaucrats to be successful in their demands for greater staffing and increases in the budget. This is not to say that bureaucrats support environmental damage, but that incentives are skewed towards budgets and staffing rather than conservation.

Likewise, because bureaucrats depend on the patronage of interest groups, policy-making is based on special interest manipulation. Management agreements compensate landowners for profits forgone due to conservationist measures. However, because these profits are not a reflection of productive efficiency but the artificial creation of agricultural support, there is an in-built tendency towards bureaucratic growth (Bowers and Cheshire, 1983). Farmers are compensated to avoid agricultural damage which would not have been viable were it not for government largesse – £2·2 billion under the CAP in 1995.

There are, of course, no powerful interest groups able to lobby for a reduction in subsidies because costs are widely dispersed across taxpayers. Farmers want to preserve their incomes and maintain inflated land values and, after initial opposition, have been quick to realise that a new coalition with the environmentalists may increase the rate of agricultural support. The NFU has long been established in the corridors of Brussels and is now joined by the ranks of the CPRE, RSPB and Friends of the Earth.

The SSSI payments direct benefits to those who are damaging, or threatening to damage, environmental sites – farmers and landowners who continue to practise good husbandry are given nothing. Thus, with the quangocratic board dominated by landowners and conservationists, bureaucrats play off both sets of interests (Marren, 1993). Some landowners continue to damage existing sites, so the bureaucrats buy off the conservationists by designating ever greater numbers of *new* SSSIs (Adams, 1993).

Conservationists argue that damage to SSSIs is the product of under-funding of management agreements (Marren, 1993). But if that is so, why have NCC bureaucrats spent time and money designating new sites, rather than using resources to protect the existing stock?

The answer is simple and predictable. The process of designation, which involves site inspection, mapping, evaluation and documentation of 'potentially damaging practices', requires more staff and an increase in the conservation budget. Thus, in the immediate aftermath of the Wildlife and Countryside Act, the NCC estimated that SSSI designation would be completed within two years, but 10 years later bureaucrats were still to complete the job (Marren, 1993, and Adams, 1993).

The government grant in aid tripled in real terms during the 1980s, from £18·8 million in 1980/81 (at 1993 prices) to £56·7 million in 1990/91 (1993 prices), of which only £7·2 million was for management agreements. Staff-related expenditure soared to reach an unprecedented 40 per cent of the total budget and the number of employees increased by 62 per cent (see Table 1), due to the explosion in site designation. Moreover, following the split in 1991, bureaucratic growth has continued apace with a 20 per cent increase in spending (from £32·6 to £39·6 million) for English Nature (EN) alone in the subsequent four years (see NCC and English Nature Annual Reports).

SSSIs are the flagship of nature conservation policy. According to the NCC (1990, p.16):

'The cornerstone of conservation practice [in Britain] is the protection and management of the most important areas for wild flora and fauna and for earth science features. The notification of SSSIs is the principal statutory means of achieving this goal.'

The importance attached to these sites is rather surprising for, as the NCC and its successor bodies themselves recognise, there are ecological grounds for questioning the validity of site designation as an appropriate means to conservation. In particular, as Soule and Simberlof (1986) suggest, there is little point in selecting isolated islands of habitat for conservation pur-

26

TABLE 1:
Budget Appropriations and Staffing at the NCC/EN,
1980/81 - 1994/95

Year	Budget (£1993 million)	Staff (Number)
1980/81	18·8	530
1981/82	19·2	535
1982/83	20·4	559
1983/84	22·3	550
1984/85	29·6	577
1985/86	36·0	689
1986/87	44·4	750
1987/88	46·7	780
1988/89	47·3	800
1989/90	49·6	820
1990/91	56·7	858
1991/92	*	*
1992/93	*	*
1993/94	*	*
1994/95	*	*
Per cent increase 1980/81 – 1994/95	202	62

* English Nature acquired 621 staff from the NCC in 1991 and by 1994/95 had recruited an extra 134 staff, making a total of 755. Remaining NCC staff were transferred to the new Scottish and Welsh bodies, so the total number in nature conservation is now over 1,000. EN spending increased from £32·6 million in 1991/92 to £39·6 million in 1994/95 (at 1993 prices).

Source: NCC/EN Annual Reports and Accounts.

poses if the surrounding countryside – that is, arable desert – is so unsuitable to the relevant flora and fauna. For birds, plants and animals to thrive, a diverse patchwork of habitats is required throughout the whole countryside. Thus, Forman and Godron (1986) highlight the importance of linkages between the different elements of the landscape such as hedges, ditches, woods and ponds. Designated sites do nothing for habitat diversity, extinction rates or the genetics of species populations (see also Hobbs, 1990). Not surprisingly, research by the British Trust for Ornithology (1991 – quoted in Felton, 1993) and the RSPB (1993/94) reports a reduction in the average clutch size of

27

linnets, a halving of the lapwing population and a corncrake population which is now so small and isolated that the species is at risk of local extinction due to random natural events.

In spite of this, an extra 1,200 SSSIs were created in England in the 14 years since the Wildlife and Countryside Act, bringing the total to 3,800 or 7 per cent of total land area (the figure for Great Britain is 6,000 or 8·5 per cent of total land area). Of course, the ever-growing number of SSSIs is not in any way reflected by a corresponding increase in the amount of high quality habitat. On the contrary, the more sites that are designated, the more devalued becomes the concept as the NCC/EN spend time designating land which is of increasingly doubtful environmental quality (Adams, 1993).

Moreover, as Table 2 shows, damage to designated sites has continued at an alarming rate. On average, each year 4 per cent of sites have been damaged, a cumulative loss of 40 per cent in 10 years, with over 80 per cent of these losses the result of agricultural practices (NCC/EN Annual Reports and Rowell, 1991).

Predictably, following vigorous lobbying by the CPRE, RSPB and EN, the latest EC Directives on Wild Birds and Habitat Conservation have produced from the DoE another wave of designations in the form of Special Protection Areas and Special Conservation Areas. As the theory of bureaucracy predicts, the more damage to environmental sites, the greater the demand for new sites and the extra budgets to 'protect' them.

Landscape Conservation

Landscape management is the arena for an array of quangocratic and ministerial agencies such as the Countryside Commission (CC), a quango attached to the DoE, and the National Park Authorities. More recently, under the provisions of the 1986 Agriculture Act, MAFF has joined the growing list of government agencies with conservation concerns.[6]

---

[6] Section 17 (1) of the Agriculture Act 1986 places a duty on MAFF to 'have regard to and endeavour to achieve a reasonable balance between the following considerations – a) the promotion and maintenance of a stable agricultural industry; b) the economic and social interests of rural areas; c) the conservation and enhancement of the natural beauty and amenity of the countryside (including its flora, fauna and geological and physiographical features) and of any features of archaeological interest there; and d) the promotion of the enjoyment of the countryside by the public.'

TABLE 2:
SSSI Losses, 1984-94

Financial Year	Number of Sites Damaged		
	Short-Term* Damage	Long-Term* Damage	Total
1984/85	161	94	255
1985/86	114	60	174
1986/87	166	70	236
1987/88	103	63	166
1988/89	160	42	202
1989/90**	261	39	300
1990/91(England only)	127	22	149
1991/92 " "	n.a.	n.a.	183
1992/93 " "	97	36	133
1993/94 " "	88	29	129

* Short-term damage refers to sites where the special interest could recover. Long-term damage is defined as a lasting or permanent loss of the site.

** There is some dispute about the data from 1988/89 to 1989/90, which suggests a substantial increase in the rate of damage. NCC argued that the data are not comparable between years because a different recording system for the earlier period understated the amount of short-term damage. Whatever the merits of this argument, the subsequent data for 1989/90 do not overstate the level of damage, even if the rate of increase is not as great as the raw figures suggest (see Adams, 1993).

Source: NCC/EN Annual Reports and Accounts.

29

These bodies control a host of countryside schemes targeted at the maintenance of traditional rural landscapes. Unlike the nature conservation bodies, most of these schemes are 'voluntary' in character. Farmers and landowners are not obliged to sign a management agreement under threat of confiscation, but the imperatives of bureaucratic control ensure that results are equally disappointing.

The ultimate example is the Countryside Commission Hedgerow Incentive Scheme which pays farmers and landowners to restore hedgerows, grubbed up due to the perversities of agricultural support. Thus, in 1992/93, 607 km. of restoration work was completed, with a further 950 km. the following year (Countryside Commission Annual Reports). Perversely, at the same time as the CC was paying farmers to restore hedgerows, three times that number (3,000 km.) were removed due to farm intensification (DoE, 1993).

Unfortunately, such absurdity is no coincidence, for it is not in the interests of the bureaucracy to lobby for reductions in agricultural support. Instead, for the sake of future staffing and budgets it is better to bribe conservationists with restoration projects, whilst farmers increase their incomes by removing hedgerows, in the knowledge that several years hence they may claim more money to put them back. Little wonder that the CC grant in aid has increased by 153 per cent in real terms over the last 15 years and staffs have more than tripled (see Table 3).

National Parks and Conservation

Consider also the activities of the 11 National Park Authorities,[7] where there is little evidence to support the view that bureaucrats

---

[7] National Parks in the United Kingdom are different in organisation to those of most other countries. In the United States, for example, the parks are owned by the state and managed by a government bureaucracy such as the US National Park Service. In the UK most of the land itself remains in private ownership, but this ownership is subject to stringent planning regulations and National Park status constitutes another form of statutory site designation. Landowners and farmers living within the bounds of the designated area are eligible for various grants and subsidies dispensed by bodies such as the Countryside Commission and the individual park authorities.

Some conservationists argue that land nationalisation as in the United States would lead to improved environmental quality in the parks. All the available evidence, however, suggests that complete government ownership makes matters considerably

TABLE 3:
Budget Appropriations and Staffing at the
Countryside Commission, 1980/81 - 1994/95

Year	Budget (£1993 million)	Staff (Number)
1980/81	n.a.	n.a.
1981/82	18·9	95
1982/83	19·7	95
1983/84	21·3	98
1984/85	20·9	100
1985/86	23·8	100
1986/87	27·0	118
1987/88	32·3	120
1988/89	27·9	128
1989/90	27·5	150
1990/91	28·1	180
1991/92	32·6	230
1992/93	46·2	300
1993/94	48·7	310
1994/95	47·7	336
Per cent increase 1980/81 – 1994/95	153	254

Source: Countryside Commission Annual Reports.

are driven by the desire for landscape conservation. On the contrary, out of a total budget of £23·4 million in 1990, on average only 21 per cent was devoted to conservation expenditures. Spending on management, administration, planning and publicity, on the other hand, amounted to 54 per cent, with the remainder spent on recreation (Stedman, 1993). This would appear to support Johnson's (1977) contention that bureaucratic agencies spend disproportionate sums on

worse, with government control amounting to bureaucratic and interest-group ownership. Baden and Leal (1990), for example, have shown in a public choice analysis of Yellowstone National Park, how massive subsidies to timber logging and recreational interests have resulted in substantial soil erosion and loss of habitat. A further difference in the UK is that National Parks are populated, farming communities. In most of the rest of the world, National Parks are wilderness and uninhabited areas.

promotional activities in the hope of attracting larger budgets and staffing in future years. Whereas private sector firms face competition and so have incentives to minimise administration and advertising costs, bureaus are quasi-monopolies and are likely to spend more on favourable publicity rather than satisfying the demands of the consumers.[8]

MAFF and Conservation

MAFF bureaucrats meanwhile have proved particularly skilful in adapting their budgetary interests to the changing political climate. In the early 1980s, when the debate about the Wildlife and Countryside Act was at its height, senior officials fought tooth and nail to avoid any challenge to the fundamentals of production support (Lowe *et al.*, 1986). However, after several years of relative budgetary decline they have adopted an increasingly close relationship with the conservationists. Through groups such as the Farming, Wildlife Advisory Group (FWAG), an alliance between farmers and conservationists, and the inclusion of the CPRE in the Agricultural Annual Review (previously monopolised by the NFU), bureaucrats have seized the opportunity to increase the agricultural budget in the name of conservation. From a position of nil 'environmental expenditure' in 1984, MAFF spending on conservation is due to reach £116 million in 1996/97.

As with the nature conservation bodies, there are few incentives for MAFF bureaucrats to encourage good stewardship because future budgets and staffing are dependent on the failure of today's schemes. Consider in this regard the programme of Environmentally Sensitive Areas (ESAs), introduced in Britain under Article 19 of EC Regulation 797/85.[9] Here it would appear that MAFF has caught the site-designating itch of the conservation quangos.

There are 22 ESAs in England (10 per cent of all farmland) covering a variety of habitats, from the moorland of the North

---

[8] Johnson uses the concept of 'bureaucratic want creation' in this regard. This is a parody of J.K Galbraith's theory of 'private sector want creation' through the use of 'manipulative' advertising (see Johnson, 1977).

[9] 25 per cent of ESA spending is 'refunded' by the EU under the so-called Agri-Environment package, the remaining 75 per cent being paid by MAFF.

Peak, to the wetlands of the Somerset Levels and the chalk hillsides of the South Downs. Most of these are considered at risk from intensification and farmers are eligible for payments and capital grants, either to 'maintain' landscape features such as hedgerows and heather or positively to 'enhance' the conservation interest.

Under the terms of these agreements, farmers may enter a part of their land into the scheme and receive payment accordingly. Thus, it is perfectly possible to receive conservation payments for one field while continuing the process of intensification on another. Indeed, some farmers might use any saving from the ESA payment to finance intensification elsewhere. Likewise it is quite legitimate to destroy habitat in order to expand production and then to claim money in future years to 'enhance' the environment by returning it to its original state.

There is little empirical evidence on the overall effect of ESA designation, but the preliminary indications confirm what one would expect, given the pattern of incentives. Thus, according to a study by the Welsh Office equivalent of MAFF, 63 per cent of farmers receiving payments in the Cambrian Mountains ESA, which is at risk from over-grazing, had no intention of improving the conservation interest (Welsh Office Agriculture Department, 1991). Likewise, in a survey of farmers in the South Downs ESA, Morris and Potter (1995) found that over 50 per cent were entering the scheme purely to increase incomes with no regard for conservation activities. Indeed, some farmers were actually compartmentalising their fields in order to maximise revenue. Arable fields which were due to be left fallow anyway were entered into the ESA in order to provide extra income, but withdrawn when the field was ready for intensive use.

Another study by Friends of the Earth, examining the Somerset Levels ESA which is at risk from drainage schemes, also found no evidence of environmental improvement. This was largely the fault of the Internal Drainage Board and the National Rivers Authority (NRA), which continue to control the water levels. It should come as no surprise that MAFF is a major source of NRA funds and the drainage boards are dominated by farmers with arable interests (FoE,1992). Once again, the bureaucracy subsidises the destruction of the landscape and then receives still more money to 'repair' it.

The pattern is very familiar: conservationists claim success in obtaining more subsidies for their personal projects, farmers happily board the new gravy train of government grants, and bureaucratic budgets grow as the multitude of schemes requires more administrators for its operation.

4. Conifers, SSSIs and the Cycle of Intervention

As the previous sections have shown, subsidised agriculture and its associated site designations are the dominant features of countryside policy, but there are other aspects of government control which, although less significant, have produced equally disappointing results. The best example is provided by a third quangocratic fiefdom – the Forestry Commission (FC – now the Forestry Authority and Forest Enterprise) – where the clash with landscape and nature conservation objectives illustrates the tendency for government intervention to degenerate into a cycle of interest-group and bureaucratic control.

Forestry Policy

Following the Ackland Report of 1917, the Forestry Commission was the first state-owned production industry created in 1919, in an attempt to restore tree cover destroyed during the First World War. The timber blockades during the Second World War provided an extra impetus for the development of a highly subsidised forestry sector and the driving force behind forestry policy following the 1940s became a massive programme of coniferous afforestation, planted by the commission itself on state-owned plantations, or via grants and tax incentives to the private sector.

As a result of these incentives, native broadleafed woodlands came under threat, for not only did the subsidies lead to planting of open spaces, but they also encouraged landowners to fell mature broadleafed woods in order to replant with coniferous monocultures. Consequently, although overall forest cover increased following the Second World War, the proportion of broadleafed woodland declined significantly (see Table 4). Ancient woodlands, which are often the richest in terms of habitat and species diversity,[1] were the principal victims and acc-

---

[1] The concept of Ancient Woodland was developed by Peterken and Rackham during the 1970s – it is defined as woodland originating before 1600 AD. In general the

TABLE 4:
The Area (kilohectares) of Major Forest Types in Britain, 1947-80

	1947	1965	1980
Mainly Coniferous High Forest	397	922	1,317
Mainly Broadleaf High Forest	380	354	564
Coppice-with Standards*	95	11	12
Coppice	50	19	28
Scrub	213	373	148
Cleared**	341	74	40
Total	1,476	1,751	2,108

* Coppice-with standards refers to the practice of coppice felling, where some of the younger trees are spared to reach full maturity, rather than rely on regeneration as in a normal coppice.

** Includes 1947 devastated woodland. The Broadleaf figure for 1947 was an all-time low, following felling during the War.

Source: Peterken and Allison (1989), reproduced in Saunders (1993).

ording to Saunders (1993), about 30 per cent of the semi-natural ancient woodland existing in 1945 had been converted to plantation by the 1980s.

Aside from the broadleaf decline, the transformation of the British uplands from wild hills and open moors to regimented armies of Sitka Spruce was the most dramatic manifestation of Forestry Commission activity. Birds of prey in particular rely on large open spaces for their hunting range and any fragmentation of moorland due to afforestation is detrimental to spectacular species such as the hen harrier and golden eagle (Goldsmith and Wood, 1983).[2] Moreover, the fertilisers used on commercial plantations produce run-off which pollutes water supplies and the thick blanket of needles beneath conifers results in soil acidification.

---

richest woods tend to be those that have been continuously wooded for the longest time (see Peterken, 1981, and Rackham, 1980).

[2] It should be noted that afforestation may not necessarily result in a total net loss of species, because coniferous planting increases the proportion of forest nesting birds such as the goldcrest, crossbill and siskin. However, most conservationists argue that any such gains are far outweighed by the loss of rare moorland habitats and their associated flora and fauna (see Goldsmith and Wood, 1983).

As the ecological effects of mass afforestation have become better known the Forestry Commission has manoeuvred and shifted its position accordingly. The initial rationale was the need to reduce reliance on imports to avoid strategic shortages and to 'help the balance of payments'. As the fallacies behind these arguments became apparent, the commission changed tack, arguing that coniferous plantations offered vital employment opportunities to rural areas; more recently the emphasis has moved to the potential for recreation.[3]

Behind all these explanations has been a powerful coalition between interest groups and the ruling bureaucracy which, as with subsidised agriculture, ensured the exclusion of forestry from the planning controls which governed alternative uses of land.[4] From the 1960s onwards, forestry in the UK became dominated by a few large forest management companies (such as Fountain and Tilhill), best able to take advantage of the subsidised régime and an incestuous relationship with the quangocratic hierarchy. There has been a continual transfer of staff between the major firms and the commission and vice versa (Stewart, 1987, p.12), with budgets and staffing dependent on the maintenance of the subsidised régime.

Moreover, the rational ignorance effect on voters is particularly strong in the case of upland afforestation, because of the relative insignificance of forestry to the economy and the simple fact that many of the most damaging practices occur in

---

[3] See Miller (1981) for a refutation of all the economic arguments advanced in favour of state forestry. For example, in response to the argument that subsidised forestry is required to avoid reliance on high priced imports in times of shortage, he replies, 'If the price of bananas promises to increase, the response is to open up new plantations in Central America, not to build subsidised green houses in the home counties' (Miller, 1981, p.25).

[4] The reader will note that the two types of land use excluded from planning control – agriculture and forestry – are also the two forms of use where the welfare of state bureaucrats is dependent on the unhindered expansion of the economic activities concerned – the greater the level of subsidised agriculture or forestry, the more bureaucrats employed and the greater the number of perks from interest groups. Indeed, the case of the Forestry Commission plantations is a classic example of the state excluding itself from the controls imposed on the rest of the population. All the activities which do fall under planning control – housing development, leisure, tourism and recreational developments – are largely provided by the private sector and are not subsidised.

sparsely populated parts of the country where there are few votes to be won.

Interest-group and bureaucratic manipulation have been well to the fore as the commission has joined the environmental bandwagon. Throughout the 1980s, the environmentalists lobbied vigorously as the continued expansion of coniferous plantations increasingly began to threaten designated SSSIs. Thus, following the amended Wildlife and Countryside Act (1985), the commission was charged with balancing the needs of landscape and nature conservation with those of the forest industry.

In 1988, the conservationists were able to claim victory as the DoE announced that large-scale coniferous plantations in England were to be discouraged and tax concessions were abolished. Significantly, there was no similar announcement with regard to Scotland. Here the patronage of FC bureaucrats and the timber firms ensured that the Scottish Office resisted any attempt towards radical reform. The reason for this was straightforward: land prices in England are much higher than in Scotland and it was in Scotland in particular that the forestry lobby had the best prospects for expansion. Thus, on the one hand the FC was able to appear 'green' by offering new broadleafed planting grants in England, whilst the timber companies and the commission itself continued the process of coniferous afforestation north of the border (Grant, 1989, pp.140-45).

The Cycle of Interventionism

It was one of the great insights of Ludwig von Mises (1936, 1981) to note the propensity of governments to engage in a self-perpetuating extension of their powers in a cycle of progressively worsening intervention. The famous clash between the forestry lobby and the NCC over the fate of the Scottish Flow Country provides the classic example of such a cycle.

The Flow Country of Caithness and Sutherland is a vast area of relatively low-lying moorland and peat-bog and is virtually the only stretch of sub-arctic tundra to be found in the British Isles. According to Lindsay (1987, p.45), 'The Flow Country ... is one of the world's outstanding ecosystems equivalent to the African Serengeti or the Brazilian Rainforest'.

38

As an open expanse of bogland, the 'Flows' are very unfavourable for forestry with over 75 per cent of the surface area classified F6 and F7 – the two lowest bands of suitability for tree planting (Mather, 1993). Ecological suitability is, however, hardly a consideration when there are huge FC subsidies on offer. Thus, in 1981 Fountain Forestry, one of the leading private timber firms, began buying up land and by 1987 around 12 per cent of the Flow had been planted with conifers (Grant, 1989).

A large part of Caithness and Sutherland had already been designated SSSI by the NCC, with rare species such as the greenshank, golden plover and the merlin, heavily reliant on the open moorland which was threatened by coniferous afforestation. Not surprisingly, the NCC, together with the RSPB, launched a counter-campaign demanding a massive extension of SSSI designations and more management agreements.

The eventual outcome of this débâcle was yet another example of bureaucratic expansionism. Following a land-use report from the Highland Regional Council in 1989, the Secretary of State for Scotland granted permission for the planting of 100,000 hectares of the Flow, whilst at the same time permitting the NCC to designate an extra 180,000 hectares of SSSI (Grant, 1989, Sinclair, 1990, and Mather, 1993). Thus, the Secretary of State succumbed to the demands of one quango to increase tree planting and to the other to provide yet more subsidies and site designations to resist the temptation of afforestation.[5]

---

[5] It has been suggested by a number of authors, for example, Mather (1993) and Goldsmith and Warren (1993), that the splitting of the NCC in 1990 was at the behest of the forestry lobby which, following the Flow Country episode, saw its interests as better served in having a weaker nature conservation body in Scotland. This view conforms to the predictions of public choice analysis, where highly focused interest groups and their supporting bureaucracies are likely to win out in any conflict with a less focused opposition. In this case, coniferous planting was only one of a number of issues which occupied the environmental lobby/ NCC, whereas subsidised conifer planting was the lifeblood of the forestry industry. It is usually the bureaucrats and interest groups with most to gain who are able to lobby and exert sufficient influence to win the day (see Benson, 1981, and Peltzman, 1976). The strength of the environmentalists with respect to agri/environment subsidies owes much to their alliance with the more narrowly focused farm lobby.

There is no accident in this tragedy of unco-ordinated intervention, for the Flow Country fiasco is but one incident in a wider pattern where bureaucratic budgets rely on policy overlap to fuel the process of growth. Thus, countryside policy is characterised by a mind-boggling list of subsidy schemes and site designations, which have produced an explosion in bureaucratic budgets. MAFF has introduced tree-planting grants to compete with the Forestry Commission, the Countryside Commission is expanding its budget for management agreements to mirror the schemes of English Nature and, all the while, MAFF bureaucrats lobby for conservation subsidies while their colleagues in Brussels refuse to challenge the nightmare of the CAP.

Each quango jealously guards its bureaucratic turf and fiercely resists any attempt at reform. The Forestry Commission has repeatedly fought off attempts at privatisation and, most recently of all, the Countryside Commission and English Nature mounted a successful campaign to avoid merger and a rationalisation of their multitudinous schemes. Bureaucrats and interest groups continue to prosper, while taxpayers and the environment continue to lose.

5. Planning and the Iron Triangle

The two preceding sections described the pattern of bureaucratic and interest group manipulation in the quango state and the proliferation of site designations and subsidy schemes which are their domain. In order to complete the analysis, it is important to return the focus to the land-use planning system, which through its own programme of designations and regulations underpins the process of bureaucratic growth, in what can only be described as an iron triangle of control between interest groups, bureaucrats and politicians.

Land Use, Subsidies and Site Designation

The underlying cause of growth in the quango state is the reliance on the three types of land use for which bureaucrats are responsible: subsidised agriculture, subsidised forestry and subsidised conservation. As the earlier sections revealed, state-supported agriculture and forestry have been damaging in their effects and conservation subsidies, so manipulated that there is little in the way of improvement. Agriculture in particular is by far the dominant land use throughout rural Britain and, as Table 5 shows, the proportion of land in agricultural use is higher than in virtually any other country in the European Union.

It is often argued that without any change to the fundamentals of price support, the only hope for the rural environment is the expansion of conservation subsidies in order to counter the effects of intensification, for example through Environmentally Sensitive Areas or the so-called Set Aside scheme (CPRE, 1992). This view is particularly amenable to the interests of bureaucrats who claim that, in the absence of British control of the CAP, the best alternative is to increase their budgets and grant-giving powers in the name of conservation. In practice, however, a more sensible alternative would be to open up the countryside to more profitable uses of land. If farmers and landholders could convert their holdings to more profitable and in many cases less damaging uses, such as small-scale housing

TABLE 5:
Percentage of Total Land Area in Agricultural
or Forestry Use in the European Community, 1994

Country	% Agriculture	% Forestry
Ireland	80·9	6·0
UK	76·8	10·0
Denmark	66·7	11·0
Italy	58·5	21·0
France	57·4	27·0
Spain	54·0	25·0
Luxembourg	49·4	32·0
Netherlands	49·7	8·0
Germany (W)	48·4	29·0
Portugal	47·6	32·0
Belgium	46·6	20·0
Greece	n.a.	n.a.

Source: European Community Maps and Office of the European
            Communities, in Holliday (1994).

developments, leisure and tourist facilities, then pressure for
intensification on the remaining agricultural land would be
reduced considerably.

Unfortunately, the prospects for rural business development
instead of intensive farming are minimal. The principal reason is
the ever-growing list of regulations imposed through the town
and country planning system, where planning bureaucrats appear
to believe that conservation is simply a matter of drawing lines
on maps. Designations such as Green Belts and Areas of
Outstanding Natural Beauty have increased apace over the last
decade (the area of green belt increased from 1·7 to 4·5 million
acres between 1979 and 1990), and over 50 per cent of the land
area is covered by controls which forbid all but agriculture and
forestry-related developments (see Table 6 and Figure 1).
Moreover, and contrary to popular opinion, the Green Belt has
had a deleterious effect on the pattern of urban development. If
cities are not allowed to expand outwards because of a tight
'green girdle', then suburban development is forced out beyond
the Green Belt, increasing the commuting distance to work and

TABLE 6:
Statutory Designations under the Town and Country Planning System in England, 1994

Designation	Area/sq.km.	% of Land Area
Green Belt	15,500	14·5
AONB	20,198	15·5
National Park	13,600	9·0
SSSI	9,750	7·0
Total	59,048	46·0

N.B. There is a slight overlap in some areas with some of the designations, and in some areas green belt boundaries have not been finalised, so all figures are an approximation. These figures do not include local authority designations such as Areas of Great Landscape Value (AGLV), Areas of Great Landscape Quality (AGLQ), Landscape Conservation Areas (LCA) or Areas of Semi-Natural Importance (ASNI), for which there are no nationwide data. In addition, 30 per cent of English farmland is graded the highest quality agricultural land by MAFF, which is considered due cause for a presumption against non-agricultural development. A further 10 per cent is designated ESA.

Source: Adapted from Cullingworth and Nadin (1994).

the demand for more roads and long-distance travel (Herington, 1984). Thus, protective designations which sound 'green' in their intent are effectively balkanising rural areas into the most environmentally destructive patterns of use.

As we saw in Section 2, the protection of 'agricultural land' was part of the intent of the 1947 system, with tenant farmers amongst the most vociferous advocates of planning controls, to redistribute development rights away from landholders. Ironically, 50 years on and with many of its members now owner-occupiers, the farming lobby has fallen foul of the very same legislation, manipulated by a new but equally destructive coalition.[1]

---

[1] Although advocating some degree of liberalisation, it should be noted that the NFU is not in favour of total deregulation. The reason for this is quite simply that the planning system artificially restricts the supply of land for non-agricultural uses and massively increases the price of land with planning permission. A modicum of

Conservationists and the 'Iron Triangle'

The farmers have been replaced as the dominant interest group in rural Britain by the conservation lobby, in particular the CPRE and Friends of the Earth. These groups are the principal representatives of middle-class newcomers, who seek to maintain rural areas for their personal consumption and resist any attempt to open up the countryside to non-agricultural uses. The term NIMBY ('Not In My Backyard') is an entirely appropriate definition of their activities, which in turn results in what might best be described as the BANANA ('Build Absolutely Nothing Anywhere Near Anybody') phenomenon.[2]

Local authority planning committees are filled with politicians, so afraid of raising the ire of nimby and banana warriors – the NIMPOO ('Not in My Period of Office' syndrome: Taylor, 1992) – that it is virtually impossible to achieve a planning permission for any non-agricultural, small business development. Irrespective of whether the conservationist hierarchy shares these nimby/banana values, it remains the case that in order to attract members, the CPRE is much more willing to tolerate a reliance on arable deserts than a more diverse, less subsidised and more wildlife friendly pattern of use.

The power of the CPRE lobby is so great that politicians have allowed nimbies to shape planning legislation to suit their own

---

liberalisation would allow farmers to make huge profits by selling their holdings as the granting of permission confers on them a monopoly 'rent' which would not be available in an unfettered land market. This is yet another example of the vested interests created by state interference in the land market.

[2] Many political science and public choice writers argue that environmental lobby groups are disadvantaged in relation to development-based groups, because the latter have a small and more easily organised potential membership, whereas the former have a large potential constituency, prone to free-riding due to the non-excludable nature of the goods for which they campaign. See, for example, Olson (1965), especially Chapters 3 and 6, and Smith (1992, pp.36-37). This argument has considerable force with respect to environmental goods such as atmospheric pollution control, where the negative effects are widely dispersed. However, it does not apply to nimby-based groups demanding site designations. Nimby groups lobby for regulations to increase property values and keep out unwanted change. These are locality based (not in my backyard) goods with a relatively small and site specific membership. Thus, it is significant that in addition to its 46,000 individual members the CPRE has almost 3,000 local residents' groups and nimby groups (average membership 200) included in the membership fold.

FIGURE 1: British Land Use Planning: Areas of Special Designation

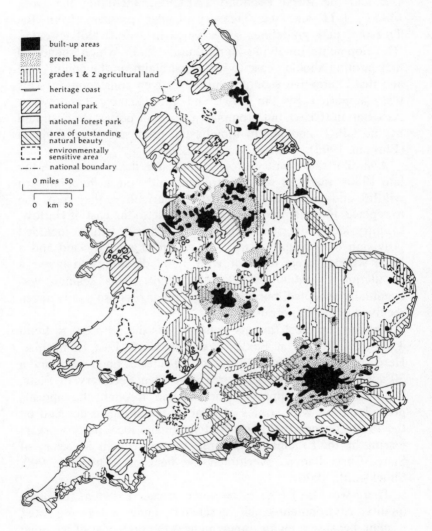

Legend:
- built-up areas
- green belt
- grades 1 & 2 agricultural land
- heritage coast
- national park
- national forest park
- area of outstanding natural beauty
- environmentally sensitive area
- national boundary

0 miles 50

0 km 50

Source: Susan Owens, 'Agricultural Land Surplus and Concern for the Countryside', in Donald Cross and Christine Whitehead (eds.), *Development and Planning 1989*, Newbury, Berks., Policy Journals, 1989, p. 36 (based on Countryside Commission, Department of the Environment and Ministry of Agriculture, Fisheries and Food sources).

narrow self-interest. Thus, in 1987, the Conservative government set up an interdepartmental working party – Alternative Land Use and the Rural Economy (ALURE), including the DoE, MAFF, DTI and the Treasury. Under pressure from the Treasury, new guidelines were issued in a draft DoE circular, 'Developments Involving Agricultural Land', which suggested that farming should cease to have first claim on the countryside and that alternative economic uses be given consideration. This was supported by the NFU and the Country Landowners Association (CLA), but prompted a storm of protest orchestrated by the CPRE and within months the proposals were dropped (Ehrman, 1990).

A similar fate awaited proposed housing developments in the late 1980s, many of which were eminently more favourable to wildlife and species diversity than the agriculture they were due to replace. For example, at Brenthall Park, to the east of Harlow, Countryside Properties proposed a scheme which included provision of a country park, restoration of meadowland and a large wooded area, together with 3,500 dwellings to house a population of 9,000 (Shucksmith, 1990). This scheme was eventually accepted, but out of 200 similar proposals only seven received planning permission.

Perhaps the most famous example was the proposal to build 4,800 new houses at Foxley Wood in North East Hampshire. Here developers planned to provide 40 acres of open space and a 30-acre water park/wetland area. The then Secretary of State, Nicholas Ridley, approved the scheme through the appeals procedure, but with armies of nimbies preparing to descend on the 1989 Conservative Party conference and local party workers tearing up their membership cards, the subsequent Secretary of State, Chris Patten, overturned the decision (Ehrman, 1990, Shucksmith, 1990).

There would, of course, be much greater potential for high-quality, environment-sensitive schemes under a less regulated system, because a major impediment is the high cost of land due to the artificially restricted supply. Land for housing is at least one hundred times the price of agricultural land without planning permission; if costs were lower, developers would be able to afford more tree planting, open-space provision and landscaping (Evans, 1988, 1991).

FIGURE 2: The Iron Triangle

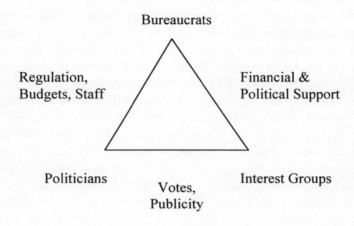

Bureaucrats

Regulation,
Budgets, Staff

Financial &
Political Support

Politicians

Votes,
Publicity

Interest Groups

The Foxley Wood announcement marked the end of any serious attempt to break the stranglehold of planning controls and, with the DoE having to make controversial and highly visible appeal decisions, the Government prepared to hand the system to the nimbies on a platter. Thus the Planning and Compensation Act (1991) reduced the ability of landowners and developers to use the appeals procedure to overturn the decisions of local planning committees by instigating a new 'presumption in favour of the plan'.

This clause (Section 54a) was inserted following an amendment drafted by the CPRE. Thereafter, planning authorities no longer needed to retain any flexibility in the system by considering proposals which do not conform to the strictures of the local development plan. Rather, all proposals are to be judged to the letter of a document which is prepared by nimby-dominated authorities.

Planning bureaucrats and quangocrats complete the 'iron triangle' of control (see Figure 2). They join with the conservation lobby in demanding greater regulation over rural land development. The greater the regulation, the more planners and bureaucrats are required and, as regulation begins to bite, farmers and landowners become ever more dependent on agricultural, forestry and conservation subsidies.

The ratchet effect of stricter planning controls and increasing bureaucratic status has been well to the fore in recent times. Planning bureaucrats in the District and County Planning Officers Societies and the Royal Town Planning Institute, and consultants and surveyors in the Royal Institution of Chartered Surveyors, lobbied vigorously with the CPRE for the new 'plan-led' system. Predictably, this has resulted in an explosion of plan-making activity and a subsequent increase in the number of local authority planners, civil servants at the DoE and yet more consultancy fees for the multitude of surveyors and lawyers needed at planning inquiries (Cullingworth and Nadin, 1994, p.59). Between 1980 and 1992, the number of local authority planners increased from 21,900 to 23,200 (computed from *Monthly Digest of Statistics*) and the length of the public inquiry procedure, where it is not uncommon for developers to pay out over £500,000 in consultancy and legal fees, increased from about seven weeks in 1988 to 22 weeks in 1992.[3]

Quangocrats at the Countryside Commission and English Nature are statutory consultees at planning inquiries and MAFF officials still retain the right of veto for any change of use resulting in the removal of 20+ hectares of agricultural land. Bureaucrats frequently seize the opportunity to lobby for more designations with the CPRE. Indeed, so incestuous is this relationship that the Countryside Commission has funded the CPRE to the tune of £120,000 over the last three years (CPRE Annual Reports 1992-94).

This is a particularly shrewd investment for the quangos because they are the bodies responsible for many of the designations – the Countryside Commission in particular designates AONBs under approval from the DoE, which are then

---

[3] As with the farmers, it must be remembered that the larger corporate developers in groups such as the Housebuilders Federation (HBF), do not favour a totally deregulated system. Planning regulations allow the larger developers to restrict entry into the market because they are the only ones able to afford the cost of planning inquiries. Likewise, restrictive planning laws artificially inflate the value of their land banks (see Evans, 1988, 1991).

given statutory protection under the planning system. Thus, the commission supports the CPRE lobbying the DoE for AONBs, which provides extra budgets to the commission, which so strangle the rural economy that farmers become ever more dependent on bureaucratic hand-outs, in turn dispensed by the commission.

Not surprisingly, then, faced with no alternative use of their land, farmers are joining ranks with the CPRE and other conservationists to lobby for an extension of MAFF, EN, CC and FC subsidies to cover all remaining rural land (NFU Annual Report 1993/94).

Property Rights, What Property Rights?

As government regulation grows, so the scope of private property rights diminishes. Indeed, to speak of private property rights in contemporary Britain is a complete misnomer. Such is the number of site designations and planning controls, there is hardly any decision regarding the use of land which may be made without reference to a bureaucratic agency. The process of nationalisation will be complete if the current campaign by the Ramblers' Association is a success. In July 1995, it persuaded Oxfordshire County Council to consider forcing the Earl of Macclesfield to allow free access to his land in the Chilterns. Ironically, much of this land is designated SSSI and is now destined for destruction under the trample of ramblers' feet. Not only do property owners no longer have a right to use their property as they see fit, but soon it would appear they will not even be allowed the fundamental right to exclude unwanted visitors. As the scope of bureaucratic decision-making and interest-group politics extends, so does the potential for government failure.

This is the inevitable consequence of the politicisation of land-use decisions, because bureaucrats and interest groups do not bear the full opportunity cost of their actions. When planners and nimbies lobby for more site designations, the benefits of control are concentrated on them, whilst the costs of continued reliance on subsidised agriculture or manipulated conservation schemes are borne by a dispersed, rationally ignorant electorate, and a long-suffering environment. Such is the history of countryside policy and it is a history of government failure.

6. A Property Rights Alternative

Given the catalogue of government failures, countryside policy is clearly ripe for reform, but the intention here is not to outline specific policy proposals. Planning controls, site designations and their associated subsidy schemes have been the focus of interest-group and bureaucratic manipulation since birth and it is difficult to conceive of any measures, short of complete abolition, which would remedy their inherent defects. Moreover, the institutional incentives which result in government failure can be guaranteed to produce vigorous resistance to even the most piecemeal of reforms. Rather, it is better to challenge the general climate of opinion which underpins the current system and in particular the belief that markets and voluntary exchange cannot be trusted with countryside conservation. To understand how markets can and do deal with these problems and to present an alternative vision for the countryside, it is vital to grasp the importance of property rights.

Property Rights in Theory

Private property rights are a fundamental requirement of a functioning market order, for the simple reason that without rights of ownership, people are unable to engage in mutually advantageous exchange (Furnbotn and Pejovich, 1972).

The exchange of property rights provides the only way for individuals to reveal the values they attach to economic resources, because the opportunity costs of particular actions are entirely subjective and known only to the individuals concerned. Only through the rejection of available alternatives may the value of choices be ascertained. Only through trade may resources obtain a valuation and, because this information is dispersed, it is the price system which makes these values known (Buchanan, 1969, and Cordato, 1992).

If property rights are clearly defined and enforced, individuals are fully aware of the actions they may take with respect to their property and must face the full opportunity cost of their decisions (Coase, 1960, Alchian and Demsetz, 1973, and Burton, 1986). Because the profitability of a project is determined by the price consumers are willing to pay, property rights provide incentives to allocate resources in the most efficient way. Consumers pay directly for the resources they use and have an incentive to monitor alternative suppliers in order to make the best choice possible, whilst entrepreneurs who succeed in satisfying the desires of their fellows may reap the rewards of their actions. These are the incentives which ensure that markets serve the wants of the people.

The property rights paradigm is equally applicable with respect to countryside conservation. If individuals, companies or voluntary bodies have private property rights in the environment, incentives will encourage the good stewardship of the resources concerned. Thus, when an environmental group holds title to a stretch of rare habitat, the wealth of its members (defined in terms of habitat conservation) is linked directly to the decisions made by the group members and if poor management decisions are made, individuals are free to place their financial contributions elsewhere (Anderson and Leal, 1991, p.20). The rôle of government in this setting is to provide the institutional framework of law which protects the property owner from force, theft or fraud.[1]

Critics argue that markets fail because the costs of defining and enforcing property rights – the transactions costs – are far too high. Although it may be easy to exclude non-payers from the benefits of a beautiful garden (for example, by erecting a high fence), it is more difficult for property owners to capture the full benefits from the preservation of scenic landscapes or important habitats. Examples of external benefits/costs mean that markets fail to reflect the true values attached to these resources by the members of society (Turner, Pearce and Bateman, 1994).

Unfortunately, what the market failure adherents seem unable to recognise is that transactions costs are also present within the

---

[1] For an account of how even these services might be provided through private initiative, see Friedman (1975), Anderson and Hill (1979), Benson (1990), Ellickson (1991), and Foldvary (1994).

political sphere. The alternative to markets is not a costless nirvana, where all externalities are internalised, but the reality of an institutional setting where transactions costs are even greater.[2] As this paper has attempted to show, so great are the costs of monitoring government decision-making, that politics degenerates into bureaucratic and interest group control. On the other hand, markets, although not 'perfect', at least provide institutional incentives which encourage innovative solutions to environmental problems.[3]

As Anderson and Leal (1991, p.21) note, any case of external benefits/costs provides fertile ground for an entrepreneur who can define and enforce property rights. A landowner who can devise ways of excluding non-payers from the benefits of a scenic view may profit from the definition of appropriate rights. If there is no demand for scenic views or habitat conservation, few will attempt to internalise their external effects, but if people are willing to pay for these goods, profits will reward those who are most successful at marketing the relevant environmental values. In other words, property rights will be defined when the marginal benefit of doing so exceeds the marginal cost (Demsetz, 1967). Property rights should be seen as part of an evolutionary process as entrepreneurs compete to provide solutions to as yet unsolved problems of environmental management (Anderson and Hill, 1975).

This approach is particularly appropriate to questions of countryside conservation for, as Foldvary (1994) has shown,

---

[2] Demsetz (1969) uses the term 'nirvana economics' to describe the position of theorists who advocate government intervention having compared existing market institutions with those of a utopian 'perfect market'. A typical example is the tendency for many neo-classical theorists to advocate government intervention on the grounds that markets fail to satisfy the criterion of 'perfect information'. Perfect information, however, can never exist in any real world setting, so the choice should always be made according to which of the alternative institutional arrangements (be it government or market) transmits information more efficiently.

[3] Many environmentalists argue that markets fail to account for so-called 'existence values', where people derive utility from the mere existence of scenic landscapes and environmental goods irrespective of whether they use them at any point during their lifetime. This argument appears spurious since there is clearly no way to decide the appropriate level of 'existence-value' provision through politics and it is far from clear why other goods such as motor cars are not deemed worthy of existence-value status.

most countryside goods categorised as non-excludable are in practice 'territorial goods' and are thus excludable by definition. The benefits of a scenic view or of attractive woodlands are present within a site specific area. Since most of these goods involve some form of leisure or recreation activity or are associated with residential environments, so long as land is privately owned, individuals must reveal their preferences in order to access the territory in question.

The private ownership of land can encourage entrepreneurs to provide countryside goods on a variety of territorial scales, ranging from small nature reserves to large country parks. Birdwatchers, wildlife lovers, walkers and recreationists may be charged entrance or user fees and because the revenue of a nature reserve depends on the number of visitors it receives, the owners have an incentive to ensure that habitats are properly conserved. Likewise, if few people are willing to pay for entry into a country park where the hills are coated with a coniferous blanket, then such practices will be discouraged.

Property rights in land might also be divided to enable the capture of environmental values. Deed restrictions and covenants may be included in contracts to ensure the preservation of scenic views and open spaces. Housing developers might purchase covenants on the lands adjacent to a development, to guarantee the preservation of a particular view or landscape feature, or alternatively plant new woodlands and restore habitats within the grounds, all of which would be reflected in higher asset prices. Profits will reward the most innovative property rights entrepreneurs as the creative forces of competition lead to a diversity of environmental schemes to suit the desires of the consumers.[4]

Property Rights in Practice

Far from being a theoretical construct, there is a wealth of evidence to support the claims of the property rights paradigm.

---

[4] Competition is used here, not in the neo-classical sense of 'perfect competition', but in the Austrian sense of rivalrous, innovative competition, the only requirement of which is free entry to challenge the established players, irrespective of the number of buyers and sellers. Government regulation is, of course, the principal barrier to free entry.

Even though government control is now so extensive, there are still many examples which show the potential for private provision if only the politicians would get out of the way.

In Britain, the bird reserves of the Wildfowl Trust provide an excellent demonstration of Foldvary's theory of territorial provision. At places such as Martin Mere (Lancashire) and Slimbridge (Gloucestershire), the Trust holds large tracts of marsh and wetlands which are a haven for waders, migrant ducks and geese. Birdwatchers and other recreationists are charged entrance fees through a turnstile system and a wide range of visitor facilities is provided (see Wildfowl Trust Annual Reports and Visitor Information).

Likewise, the RSPB, with an annual budget of £30 million, is the owner of 118 nature reserves and runs a wide range of schemes to encourage birdwatching, with members given free entry into the reserves (RSPB, 1993/94). In the United States, the Audubon Society owns a number of wildlife/country parks such as the Rainey Wildlife Sanctuary in Louisiana, which covers some 28,000 acres of marshland and swamp, and is home to thousands of snow geese and swamp creatures such as mink and alligators (Taylor, 1992).

Consider also the successful provision of private park services in the United States by the North Maine Woods Inclusive, a company formed through an association of 20 landowners. The North Maine Woods manages recreational activities in a 2·8 million acre park (an area half the size of Wales) and provides camping and other leisure facilities. Entrance to the park is controlled through 17 checkpoints and access roads, with fees charged for visitors and campers according to the length of stay (Anderson and Leal, 1991, p.69).

The activities of the National Trust also confirm the potential for private provision. Ever since the first purchase of 14 acres at Barras Head near Tintagel in 1897, the National Trust has purchased historic monuments and areas of natural beauty and now holds title to over 777 sq. km. of countryside (Cullingworth and Nadin, 1994). Through a variety of techniques such as entrance fees and charges for car parking, the Trust is very successful in the marketing of environmental values.

Some writers of late have criticised the National Trust for spending too much time looking after its buildings rather than the landscapes which it owns (Micklewright, 1993). But if this criticism is valid, there is all the more need to deregulate the countryside to encourage alternative suppliers of countryside goods. The planning system and the paraphernalia of site designation act to 'crowd out' alternative forms of supply and thus create a quasi-monopoly status for the remaining private suppliers.

The experience of the US Nature Conservancy illustrates the enormous potential for property rights/environmental entrepreneurship. As Anderson and Leal (1991, p.3) report, the Conservancy obtains tracts of land for habitat conservation and then trades these sites (with restrictive covenants attached) in order to accumulate more important habitats. Thus, when the Wisconsin Nature Conservancy was approached concerning the sale of some its beachfront property, the Conservancy traded the site (with covenants) and used the money to purchase a much larger parcel of rocky hillside in Northern Wisconsin, which allowed the protection of a whole watershed containing many endangered plant species.

Restrictive covenants have a long history of use in the urban areas of Britain. Many parts of Westminster, Bloomsbury, Hampstead, Oxford and Cambridge include private covenants designed to preserve their character and to maintain property values (West, 1969). Before the advent of the planning system, the National Trust used the covenant approach quite widely (Clapp, 1994, pp.123-37), so there is clearly no reason why this approach cannot successfully be applied to countryside conservation.[5]

Development interests are well aware of the advantages of attempting to market environmental values. The demand for environmental amenities is income elastic and there are profits to be made for those who can capture environmental quality in their schemes.[6] Thus, the Brenthall Park development referred to

---

[5] For further discussion on the operation of restrictive covenants in the American context, see Siegan (1972), Ellickson (1973), and Fischel (1985).

[6] Income elasticity refers to the phenomenon where as incomes rise, the demand for a particular good or service also rises. As people become richer they tend to place a higher premium on environmental quality, so environmental goods are often defined as income elastic.

in Section 5 was an attempt by a housing developer to capture the value of restored meadowland, woodland and open countryside. All of these amenities were encompassed within the site, so residential consumers had no choice but to reveal their preferences for environmental quality in the purchase price of the houses. A similar principle lies behind the successful tourist developments of Center Parcs, where a wide range of leisure, recreation and hotel facilities is provided within thickly wooded sites.

The great virtue of property rights solutions is that people must face the full opportunity cost of their actions and are able to reap the rewards of good stewardship and to be penalised for poor stewardship. Farmers would not be able to claim greater subsidies regardless of their success in conserving the landscape, and nimbies would be unable to balkanise the countryside into a single pattern of use, unless they were prepared to pay the full price of doing so.

Nothing could be further removed from the bureaucratic method which has come to dominate countryside policy in the UK. The true potential for property rights entrepreneurship will never be realised under anything resembling the present system, for the simple reason that there are virtually no property rights to be entrepreneurial with. Entrepreneurs will not provide country parks if consumers are told that compulsory National Park designation is a guarantee of free access. Environmental groups will not seek to accumulate more habitats and landscape features through the use of covenants if they can lobby for Sites of Special Scientific Interest, and developers will be less minded to capture environmental quality in their schemes if planners and nimbies continue to lobby for Green Belts.

Every planning control, site designation and subsidy scheme removes from the individual the responsibility for his or her actions and transfers them to the unaccountable realm of the bureaucrat, the interest group and the politician. The failure of countryside policy is not the product of markets, but the inevitable result of their absence.

7. Conclusion

At the outset, this paper discussed the importance of institutions and two competing visions of government intervention in the countryside. The dominant vision sees markets and private property as the cause of countryside destruction and advocates a solution based on bureaucratic decision-making by benevolent government planners. The evidence presented here contradicts this approach and suggests that perverse incentives in the political process are symptomatic of 'government failure' on a massive scale. It would not be an exaggeration to state that almost every act of countryside destruction has resulted from the bureaucratic desire to increase budgets and the political desire to buy votes. The dominant interests have changed over time but the pattern of environmental failure has persisted throughout.

The inescapable conclusion of this paper is the need to establish an alternative institutional framework for countryside management. Such a framework can be provided only through the tried and tested method of private property rights and the market order. These are the institutions which reward those who care for the countryside and penalise those who do not. The desires of the people for greater environmental quality are being thwarted by an outdated system which deprives them of the means through which to improve their environment and to be rewarded accordingly. The rôle of government in a free society is to protect the right to private property and not to engage in its confiscation.

If countryside conservation is the aim, it is time to dismantle the vast paraphernalia of planning and the quango state and to return to the democracy of the market.

The Countryside Alphabet

Quangos and Bureaucracies

CC	Countryside Commission
CCW	Countryside Council for Wales
DoE	Department of the Environment
EN	English Nature
FC	Forestry Commission
LPA	Local Planning Authority
MAFF	Ministry of Agriculture Fisheries and Food
NCC	Nature Conservancy Council (until 1990)
NRA	National Rivers Authority
RDC	Rural Development Commission
SNH	Scottish Natural Heritage

Site Designations

AGLQ	Area of Great Landscape Quality
AGLV	Area of Great Landscape Value
AONB	Area of Outstanding Natural Beauty
ASI	Area of Scientific Interest
ASSI	Area of Special Scientific Interest
ESA	Environmentally Sensitive Area
GB	Green Belt
HC	Heritage Coast
LCA	Local Conservation Area
LNR	Local Nature Reserve
NNR	National Nature Reserve
NP	National Park
NSA	National Scenic Area
RS	Ramsar Site
SSSI	Site of Special Scientific Interest
SCA	Special Conservation Area
SPA	Special Protection Area

Interest Groups

CLA	Country Landowners Association
CPOS	County Planning Officers Society
CPRE	Council for the Protection of Rural England
DPOS	District Planning Officers Society
FWAG	Farming, Wildlife Advisory Group
FoE	Friends of the Earth
HBF	Housebuilders Federation
NFU	National Farmers Union
RA	Ramblers Association
RICS	Royal Institution of Chartered Surveyors
RSNC	Royal Society for Nature Conservation
RSPB	Royal Society for the Protection of Birds
RTPI	Royal Town Planning Institute

Anti-Development Acronyms

BANANA	Build Absolutely Nothing Anywhere Near Anybody
NIMBY	Not in My Backyard
NIMPOO	Not in My Period of Office

References/Bibliography

Adams, W. (1993): 'Places for Nature: Protected Areas in British Nature Conservation', in Goldsmith and Warren (1993), *op. cit.*

Alchian, A., and H. Demsetz (1973): 'The Property Rights Paradigm', *Journal of Economic History*, Vol.3, No.1, pp.16-27.

Anderson, T. (1982): 'New Resource Economics : Old Ideas and New Applications', *American Journal of Agricultural Economics*, Vol.64, pp.928-34.

Anderson, T., and P.J. Hill (1975): 'The Evolution of Property Rights: A Study of the American West', *Journal of Law and Economics*, April, pp.168-79.

_____ (1979): 'An American Experiment in Anarcho-Capitalism: The Not So Wild, Wild West', *Journal of Libertarian Studies*, Vol.3, pp.9-29.

Anderson, T., and D. Leal (1991): *Free Market Environmentalism*, San Francisco: Pacific Research Institute for Public Policy.

Baden, J., and R. Fort (1980): 'Natural Resources and Bureaucratic Predators', *Policy Review*, Winter, pp.69-82.

Baden, J., and R. Stroup (1981): *Bureaucracy versus the Environment*, Ann Arbor: University of Michigan Press.

Baden, J., and D. Leal (1990): *The Yellowstone Primer*, San Francisco: Pacific Research Institute for Public Policy.

Barton, P.M., and G.P. Buckley (1983): 'The Status and Protection of Sites of Special Scientific Interest in South East England', *Biological Conservation*, Vol.27, pp.213-42.

Baumol, W., and W. Oates (1975): *The Theory of Environmental Policy*, Englewood Cliffs, NJ: Prentice-Hall.

Benson, B.L. (1981): 'Land Use Regulation: A Supply and Demand Analysis of Changing Property Rights', *Journal of Libertarian Studies*, Vol.5, pp.435-51.

_____ (1990): *The Enterprise of Law*, San Francisco: Pacific Research Institute for Public Policy.

Blais, A., and S. Dion (1991): *The Budget Maximizing Bureaucrat: Appraisals and Evidence*, Pittsburgh: University of Pittsburgh Press.

Blowers, A. (ed.) (1994): *Planning for a Sustainable Environment*, London: Town and Country Planning Association/Earthscan.

Body, R. (1983): *Agriculture: The Triumph and the Shame*, Aldershot, Hants.: Temple/Smith/Gower.

Bowers, J.K., and P. Cheshire (1983): *Agriculture, The Countryside and Landuse*, London: University Paperbacks, Methuen.

Buchanan, J.M. (1969): *Cost and Choice*, Chicago: Markham Publishing.

Buchanan, J.M., *et al.* (1978): *The Economics of Politics*, IEA Readings No.18, London: Institute of Economic Affairs.

Buchanan, J.M., and G. Tullock (1982): *Towards a Theory of the Rent Seeking Society*, Austin: Texas A&M Press.

Burton, J. (1986): 'Externalities, Property Rights and Public Policy: Private Property Rights or the Spoilation of Nature', in S.N.S. Cheung (1986), *op. cit.*

Burton, T. (1991): 'The Planning and Compensation Bill', *Ecos*.

Cheung, S.N.S. (1986): *The Myth of Social Cost*, Hobart Paper No.82, London: Institute of Economic Affairs.

Clapp, B.W. (1994): *An Environmental History of Britain*, London: Longman.

Coase, R.H. (1960): 'The Problem of Social Cost', *Journal of Law and Economics*, Vol.3, pp.1-44.

Cordato, R.E. (1992): *Welfare Economics and Externalities in an Open-Ended Universe: A Modern Austrian Perspective*, London: Kluwer Academic Press.

Council for the Protection of Rural England (1992): *The CAP That Doesn't Fit*, London: CPRE.

Cullingworth, J.M., and V. Nadin (1994): *Town and Country Planning in Britain*, London: Routledge.

Deacon, R.T., and M.B. Johnson (eds.) (1985): *Forestlands: Public or Private?*, Cambridge, MA: Ballinger.

Demsetz, H. (1967): 'Towards a Theory of Property Rights', *American Economic Review*, Vol.57, pp.347-59.

_____ (1969): 'Information and Efficiency: Another Viewpoint', *Journal of Law and Economics*, Vol.12, No.1, pp.1-22.

Department of the Environment (1993): *Countryside Survey*, London: HMSO.

Dunleavy, P. (1991): *Democracy, Bureaucracy and Public Choice*, London: Harvester/Wheatsheaf.

Downs, A. (1957): *An Economic Theory of Democracy*, New York: Harper & Row.

Ellickson, R. (1973): 'Alternatives to Zoning: Covenants, Nuisance Rules and Fines as Land Use Controls', *University of Chicago Law Review*, Vol.40, pp.681-782.

_____ (1991): *Order Without Law*, Cambridge, MA: Harvard University Press.

Ehrman, R. (1990): *Nimbyism: The Disease and the Cure*, London: Centre for Policy Studies.

Evans, A.W. (1988): *No Room, No Room!*, Occasional Paper No.79, London: Institute of Economic Affairs.

_____ (1991): 'Rabbit Hutches on Postage Stamps: Planning, Development and Political Economy', *Urban Studies*, Vol.28, No.6, pp.853-70.

Felton, M. (1993): 'Achieving Nature Conservation Objectives: Problems and Opportunities with Economics', *Journal of Environmental Planning and Management*, Vol.36, No.1.

Fischel, W. (1985): *The Economics of Zoning Laws*, Baltimore: John Hopkins University Press.

Foldvary, F. (1994): *Public Goods and Private Communities*, London: The Locke Institute, Edward Elgar.

Forman, R.T., and M. Godron (1986): *Landscape Ecology*, Chichester: Wiley.

Formaini, R. (1991): *The Myth of Scientific Public Policy*, New York: Transaction Books.

Friends of the Earth (1992): *Environmentally Sensitive Areas*, London: FoE.

Friedman, D. (1975): *The Machinery of Freedom: Guide to a Radical Capitalism*, La Salle: Open Court.

Furnbotn, E.G., and S. Pejovich (1972): 'Property Rights and Economic Theory: A Survey of the Recent Literature', *Journal of Economic Literature*, Vol.10, pp.1,137-62.

Goldsmith, F.B., and A. Warren (eds.) (1993): *Conservation in Progress*, Chichester: Wiley.

Goldsmith, F.B., and J.B. Wood (1983): *The Ecological Effects of Upland Afforestation*, in A. Warren and F.B. Goldsmith (1983), *op. cit.*

Grant, M., and D. Heap (1991): *Encyclopaedia of Planning Law and Practice*, London: Sweet & Maxwell.

Grant, W. (1989): *Pressure Groups, Politics and Democracy in Britain*, London: Allen & Unwin.

Hayek, F.A. (1948/1945a): 'The Use of Knowledge in Society', reprinted from *American Economic Review*, Vol.35, No.4, pp.519-30, in *Individualism and Economic Order*, South Bend, Indiana: Gateway Editions.

Herington, J.M. (1984): *The Outer City*, London: Paul Chapman.

Hobbs, R.J. (1990): 'Nature Conservation: The Role of Corridors', *Ambio*, Vol.19, No.2, pp.94-95.

Holliday, J. (1994): 'Ecosystems and Natural Resources', in Blowers (ed.) (1994) *op. cit.*

Howarth, R.W. (1990): *Farming for Farmers*, Hobart Paperback No.20 (2nd edn.), London: Institute of Economic Affairs.

Johnson, M.B. (1977): 'Planning Without Prices : A Discussion of Land Use Regulation Without Compensation', in Siegan (1977), *op. cit.*

Kirzner, I.M. (1992): *The Meaning of Market Process*, London: Routledge.

Lewis, R. (ed.) (1992): *Rethinking the Environment*, London: Adam Smith Institute.

Libecap, G. (1981): *Locking Up the Range*, San Francisco: Pacific Research Institute for Public Policy.

_____ (1989): *Contracting for Property Rights*, Cambridge: Cambridge University Press.

Lindsay, R.A. (1987): 'The Great Flow: An International Responsibility', *New Scientist*, No.1542, 8 January, pp.371-84.

Lowe, P. *et al.* (1986): *Countryside Conflicts*, Aldershot: Temple/Smith/Gower.

Marren, P. (1993): 'The Siege of the NCC', in Goldsmith and Warren (1993), *op. cit.*

Mather, A.S. (1993): 'Protected Areas in the Periphery: Conservation and Controversy in Northern Scotland', *Journal of Rural Studies*, Vol.9, No.4, pp.371-84.

Micklewright, S. (1993): 'The Voluntary Movement', in Goldsmith and Warren (1993), *op. cit.*

Miller, R. (1981): *State Forestry for the Axe*, Hobart Paper No.91, London: Institute of Economic Affairs.

Mises, L. von (1936, 1981): *Socialism : An Economic and Sociological Analysis*, Indianapolis: Liberty Classics.

Morris, C., and C. Potter (1995): 'Recruiting the New Conservationists: Farmers' Adoption of Agri-Environment Schemes in the UK', *Journal of Rural Studies*, Vol.11, No.1, pp.51-63.

Munton, R. (1983): 'Agriculture and Conservation: What Room for Compromise?', in Warren and Goldsmith (1983), *op. cit.*

Niskanen, W.A. (1971): *Bureaucracy and Representative Government*, Chicago: Aldine Atherton.

North, D. (1990): *Institutions, Institutional Change and Economic Performance*, Cambridge: Cambridge University Press.

Olson, M. (1965): *The Logic of Collective Action*, Cambridge, MA: Harvard University Press.

Peltzman, S. (1976): 'Toward a More General Theory of Economic Regulation', *Journal of Law and Economics*, Vol.19, No.3, pp.211-48.

Peterken, G.F. (1981): *Woodland Conservation and Management*, London: Chapman & Hall.

Peterken, G.F., and H. Allison (1989): *Woods, Trees and Hedges: A Review of Changes in the British Countryside*, Focus on Nature Conservation No.22, Peterborough: Nature Conservancy Council.

Rackham, O. (1980): *Ancient Woodland: Its History, Vegetation and Uses in England*, London: Edward Arnold.

Radnitzky, G., and H. Bouillon (1993): *Government: Servant or Master?*, Amsterdam, Atlantic: Rodopi.

Rowell, T.A. (1991): *SSSIs : A Health Check*, London: Wildlife Link.

Royal Society for the Protection of Birds (1993): *Conservation Review*, The Lodge, Sandy, Beds.: RSPB.

Saunders, G. (1993): 'Woodland Conservation in Britain', in Goldsmith and Warren (1993), *op. cit.*

Seldon, A. (1993): 'Politicians: For or Against the People?', in Radnitzky and Bouillon (1993), *op. cit.*

Shucksmith, M. (1990): *Housebuilding in Britain's Countryside*, London: Routledge.

Siegan, B. (1972): *Land Use Without Zoning*, Massachusetts: Lexington Books.

Siegan, B. (ed.) (1977): *Planning Without Prices*, Massachusetts: Lexington Books.

Sinclair, J. (1990): *Taking the Land in Hand*, London: Hebden Royd.

Smith, Z. (1992): *The Environmental Policy Paradox*, New Jersey: Prentice Hall.

Soule, M.E., and D. Simberlof (1986): 'What Do Genetics and Ecology Tell Us About the Design of Nature Reserves?'', *Biological Conservation*, Vol.35, pp.19-40.

Stedman, N. (1993): 'Conservation in National Parks', in Goldsmith and Warren (1993), *op. cit.*

Stewart, P.J (1987): *Growing Against The Grain*, London: CPRE.

Stigler, G. (1975): *The Citizen and the State*, Chicago: University of Chicago Press.

Taylor, R. (1992): 'Market and Non-Market Environmental Policy', in Lewis (ed.) (1992), *op. cit.*

_____ (1992): 'Market Environmentalism in Practice', in Lewis (ed.) (1992), *op. cit.*

Tullock, G. (1989): *The Economics of Special Privilege and Rent Seeking*, London: Kluwer Academic Press.

Turner, R.K., D. Pearce and I. Bateman (1994): *Environmental Economics*, London: Harvester/Wheatsheaf.

Warren, A., and F.B. Goldsmith (1983): *Conservation in Perspective*, Chichester: Wiley.

West, W.A. (1969): *Private Capital for New Towns*, Occasional Paper No.28, London: Institute of Economic Affairs.

Welsh Office Agriculture Department (1991): *ESAs Wales: Socio-Economic Aspects of Designation – Interim Report*, London: WOAD – Welsh Office.